This Address Book Belongs To:

Name	
Address	
Phone	
Email	

Name	
Address	
Phone	
Work Phone/Fax	
Email	
Notable Date(s)	

Name	
Address	
Phone	
Work Phone/Fax	
Email	
Notable Date(s)	

Name	
Address	
Phone	
Work Phone/Fax	
Email	
Notable Date(s)	

Name	
Address	
Phone	
Work Phone/Fax	
Email	
Notable Date(s)	

Name	
Address	
Phone	
Work Phone/Fax	
Email	
Notable Date(s)	

Name	
Address	
Phone	
Work Phone/Fax	
Email	
Notable Date(s)	

Name	
Address	
Phone	
Work Phone/Fax	
Email	
Notable Date(s)	

Name	
Address	
Phone	
Work Phone/Fax	
Email	
Notable Date(s)	

Name	
Address	
Phone	
Work Phone/Fax	
Email	
Notable Date(s)	

A

Name	
Address	
Phone	
Work Phone/Fax	
Email	
Notable Date(s)	

Name	
Address	
Phone	
Work Phone/Fax	
Email	
Notable Date(s)	

Name	
Address	
Phone	
Work Phone/Fax	
Email	
Notable Date(s)	

Name	
Address	
Phone	
Work Phone/Fax	
Email	
Notable Date(s)	

Name	
Address	
Phone	
Work Phone/Fax	
Email	
Notable Date(s)	

Name	
Address	
Phone	
Work Phone/Fax	
Email	
Notable Date(s)	

B

Name	
Address	
Phone	
Work Phone/Fax	
Email	
Notable Date(s)	

Name	
Address	
Phone	
Work Phone/Fax	
Email	
Notable Date(s)	

Name	
Address	
Phone	
Work Phone/Fax	
Email	
Notable Date(s)	

Name	
Address	
Phone	
Work Phone/Fax	
Email	
Notable Date(s)	

Name	
Address	
Phone	
Work Phone/Fax	
Email	
Notable Date(s)	

Name	
Address	
Phone	
Work Phone/Fax	
Email	
Notable Date(s)	

B

Name	
Address	
Phone	
Work Phone/Fax	
Email	
Notable Date(s)	

Name	
Address	
Phone	
Work Phone/Fax	
Email	
Notable Date(s)	

Name	
Address	
Phone	
Work Phone/Fax	
Email	
Notable Date(s)	

Name	
Address	
Phone	
Work Phone/Fax	
Email	
Notable Date(s)	

Name	
Address	
Phone	
Work Phone/Fax	
Email	
Notable Date(s)	

Name	
Address	
Phone	
Work Phone/Fax	
Email	
Notable Date(s)	

C

Name	
Address	
Phone	
Work Phone/Fax	
Email	
Notable Date(s)	

Name	
Address	
Phone	
Work Phone/Fax	
Email	
Notable Date(s)	

Name	
Address	
Phone	
Work Phone/Fax	
Email	
Notable Date(s)	

Name	
Address	
Phone	
Work Phone/Fax	
Email	
Notable Date(s)	

Name	
Address	
Phone	
Work Phone/Fax	
Email	
Notable Date(s)	

Name	
Address	
Phone	
Work Phone/Fax	
Email	
Notable Date(s)	

C

Name	
Address	
Phone	
Work Phone/Fax	
Email	
Notable Date(s)	

Name	
Address	
Phone	
Work Phone/Fax	
Email	
Notable Date(s)	

Name	
Address	
Phone	
Work Phone/Fax	
Email	
Notable Date(s)	

Name	
Address	
Phone	
Work Phone/Fax	
Email	
Notable Date(s)	

Name	
Address	
Phone	
Work Phone/Fax	
Email	
Notable Date(s)	

Name	
Address	
Phone	
Work Phone/Fax	
Email	
Notable Date(s)	

D

Name	
Address	
Phone	
Work Phone/Fax	
Email	
Notable Date(s)	

Name	
Address	
Phone	
Work Phone/Fax	
Email	
Notable Date(s)	

Name	
Address	
Phone	
Work Phone/Fax	
Email	
Notable Date(s)	

Name	
Address	
Phone	
Work Phone/Fax	
Email	
Notable Date(s)	

Name	
Address	
Phone	
Work Phone/Fax	
Email	
Notable Date(s)	

Name	
Address	
Phone	
Work Phone/Fax	
Email	
Notable Date(s)	

D

Name	
Address	
Phone	
Work Phone/Fax	
Email	
Notable Date(s)	

Name	
Address	
Phone	
Work Phone/Fax	
Email	
Notable Date(s)	

Name	
Address	
Phone	
Work Phone/Fax	
Email	
Notable Date(s)	

Name	
Address	
Phone	
Work Phone/Fax	
Email	
Notable Date(s)	

Name	
Address	
Phone	
Work Phone/Fax	
Email	
Notable Date(s)	

Name	
Address	
Phone	
Work Phone/Fax	
Email	
Notable Date(s)	

Name	
Address	
Phone	
Work Phone/Fax	
Email	
Notable Date(s)	

Name	
Address	
Phone	
Work Phone/Fax	
Email	
Notable Date(s)	

Name	
Address	
Phone	
Work Phone/Fax	
Email	
Notable Date(s)	

Name	
Address	
Phone	
Work Phone/Fax	
Email	
Notable Date(s)	

Name	
Address	
Phone	
Work Phone/Fax	
Email	
Notable Date(s)	

Name	
Address	
Phone	
Work Phone/Fax	
Email	
Notable Date(s)	

Name	
Address	
Phone	
Work Phone/Fax	
Email	
Notable Date(s)	
Name	
Address	
Phone	
Work Phone/Fax	
Email	
Notable Date(s)	
Name	
Address	
Phone	
Work Phone/Fax	
Email	
Notable Date(s)	

Name	
Address	
Phone	
Work Phone/Fax	
Email	
Notable Date(s)	

Name	
Address	
Phone	
Work Phone/Fax	
Email	
Notable Date(s)	

Name	
Address	
Phone	
Work Phone/Fax	
Email	
Notable Date(s)	

Name	
Address	
Phone	
Work Phone/Fax	
Email	
Notable Date(s)	

Name	
Address	
Phone	
Work Phone/Fax	
Email	
Notable Date(s)	

Name	
Address	
Phone	
Work Phone/Fax	
Email	
Notable Date(s)	

Name	
Address	
Phone	
Work Phone/Fax	
Email	
Notable Date(s)	

Name	
Address	
Phone	
Work Phone/Fax	
Email	
Notable Date(s)	

Name	
Address	
Phone	
Work Phone/Fax	
Email	
Notable Date(s)	

Name	
Address	
Phone	
Work Phone/Fax	
Email	
Notable Date(s)	

Name	
Address	
Phone	
Work Phone/Fax	
Email	
Notable Date(s)	

Name	
Address	
Phone	
Work Phone/Fax	
Email	
Notable Date(s)	

G

Name	
Address	
Phone	
Work Phone/Fax	
Email	
Notable Date(s)	

Name	
Address	
Phone	
Work Phone/Fax	
Email	
Notable Date(s)	

Name	
Address	
Phone	
Work Phone/Fax	
Email	
Notable Date(s)	

G

Name	
Address	
Phone	
Work Phone/Fax	
Email	
Notable Date(s)	

Name	
Address	
Phone	
Work Phone/Fax	
Email	
Notable Date(s)	

Name	
Address	
Phone	
Work Phone/Fax	
Email	
Notable Date(s)	

G

Name	
Address	
Phone	
Work Phone/Fax	
Email	
Notable Date(s)	

Name	
Address	
Phone	
Work Phone/Fax	
Email	
Notable Date(s)	

Name	
Address	
Phone	
Work Phone/Fax	
Email	
Notable Date(s)	

G

Name	
Address	
Phone	
Work Phone/Fax	
Email	
Notable Date(s)	

Name	
Address	
Phone	
Work Phone/Fax	
Email	
Notable Date(s)	

Name	
Address	
Phone	
Work Phone/Fax	
Email	
Notable Date(s)	

Name	
Address	
Phone	
Work Phone/Fax	
Email	
Notable Date(s)	

Name	
Address	
Phone	
Work Phone/Fax	
Email	
Notable Date(s)	

Name	
Address	
Phone	
Work Phone/Fax	
Email	
Notable Date(s)	

Name	
Address	
Phone	
Work Phone/Fax	
Email	
Notable Date(s)	
Name	
Address	
Phone	
Work Phone/Fax	
Email	
Notable Date(s)	
Name	
Address	
Phone	
Work Phone/Fax	
Email	
Notable Date(s)	

Name	
Address	
Phone	
Work Phone/Fax	
Email	
Notable Date(s)	

Name	
Address	
Phone	
Work Phone/Fax	
Email	
Notable Date(s)	

Name	
Address	
Phone	
Work Phone/Fax	
Email	
Notable Date(s)	

Name	
Address	
Phone	
Work Phone/Fax	
Email	
Notable Date(s)	

Name	
Address	
Phone	
Work Phone/Fax	
Email	
Notable Date(s)	

Name	
Address	
Phone	
Work Phone/Fax	
Email	
Notable Date(s)	

I

Name	
Address	
Phone	
Work Phone/Fax	
Email	
Notable Date(s)	

Name	
Address	
Phone	
Work Phone/Fax	
Email	
Notable Date(s)	

Name	
Address	
Phone	
Work Phone/Fax	
Email	
Notable Date(s)	

I

Name	
Address	
Phone	
Work Phone/Fax	
Email	
Notable Date(s)	

Name	
Address	
Phone	
Work Phone/Fax	
Email	
Notable Date(s)	

Name	
Address	
Phone	
Work Phone/Fax	
Email	
Notable Date(s)	

I

Name	
Address	
Phone	
Work Phone/Fax	
Email	
Notable Date(s)	

Name	
Address	
Phone	
Work Phone/Fax	
Email	
Notable Date(s)	

Name	
Address	
Phone	
Work Phone/Fax	
Email	
Notable Date(s)	

I

Name	
Address	
Phone	
Work Phone/Fax	
Email	
Notable Date(s)	

Name	
Address	
Phone	
Work Phone/Fax	
Email	
Notable Date(s)	

Name	
Address	
Phone	
Work Phone/Fax	
Email	
Notable Date(s)	

J

Name	
Address	
Phone	
Work Phone/Fax	
Email	
Notable Date(s)	

Name	
Address	
Phone	
Work Phone/Fax	
Email	
Notable Date(s)	

Name	
Address	
Phone	
Work Phone/Fax	
Email	
Notable Date(s)	

J

Name	
Address	
Phone	
Work Phone/Fax	
Email	
Notable Date(s)	

Name	
Address	
Phone	
Work Phone/Fax	
Email	
Notable Date(s)	

Name	
Address	
Phone	
Work Phone/Fax	
Email	
Notable Date(s)	

J

Name	
Address	
Phone	
Work Phone/Fax	
Email	
Notable Date(s)	

Name	
Address	
Phone	
Work Phone/Fax	
Email	
Notable Date(s)	

Name	
Address	
Phone	
Work Phone/Fax	
Email	
Notable Date(s)	

J

Name	
Address	
Phone	
Work Phone/Fax	
Email	
Notable Date(s)	

Name	
Address	
Phone	
Work Phone/Fax	
Email	
Notable Date(s)	

Name	
Address	
Phone	
Work Phone/Fax	
Email	
Notable Date(s)	

Name	
Address	
Phone	
Work Phone/Fax	
Email	
Notable Date(s)	

Name	
Address	
Phone	
Work Phone/Fax	
Email	
Notable Date(s)	

Name	
Address	
Phone	
Work Phone/Fax	
Email	
Notable Date(s)	

Name	
Address	
Phone	
Work Phone/Fax	
Email	
Notable Date(s)	

Name	
Address	
Phone	
Work Phone/Fax	
Email	
Notable Date(s)	

Name	
Address	
Phone	
Work Phone/Fax	
Email	
Notable Date(s)	

Name	
Address	
Phone	
Work Phone/Fax	
Email	
Notable Date(s)	

Name	
Address	
Phone	
Work Phone/Fax	
Email	
Notable Date(s)	

Name	
Address	
Phone	
Work Phone/Fax	
Email	
Notable Date(s)	

Name	
Address	
Phone	
Work Phone/Fax	
Email	
Notable Date(s)	

Name	
Address	
Phone	
Work Phone/Fax	
Email	
Notable Date(s)	

Name	
Address	
Phone	
Work Phone/Fax	
Email	
Notable Date(s)	

L

Name	
Address	
Phone	
Work Phone/Fax	
Email	
Notable Date(s)	

Name	
Address	
Phone	
Work Phone/Fax	
Email	
Notable Date(s)	

Name	
Address	
Phone	
Work Phone/Fax	
Email	
Notable Date(s)	

Name	
Address	
Phone	
Work Phone/Fax	
Email	
Notable Date(s)	
Name	
Address	
Phone	
Work Phone/Fax	
Email	
Notable Date(s)	
Name	
Address	
Phone	
Work Phone/Fax	
Email	
Notable Date(s)	

Name	
Address	
Phone	
Work Phone/Fax	
Email	
Notable Date(s)	

Name	
Address	
Phone	
Work Phone/Fax	
Email	
Notable Date(s)	

Name	
Address	
Phone	
Work Phone/Fax	
Email	
Notable Date(s)	

Name	
Address	
Phone	
Work Phone/Fax	
Email	
Notable Date(s)	

Name	
Address	
Phone	
Work Phone/Fax	
Email	
Notable Date(s)	

Name	
Address	
Phone	
Work Phone/Fax	
Email	
Notable Date(s)	

Name	
Address	
Phone	
Work Phone/Fax	
Email	
Notable Date(s)	

Name	
Address	
Phone	
Work Phone/Fax	
Email	
Notable Date(s)	

Name	
Address	
Phone	
Work Phone/Fax	
Email	
Notable Date(s)	

Name	
Address	
Phone	
Work Phone/Fax	
Email	
Notable Date(s)	

Name	
Address	
Phone	
Work Phone/Fax	
Email	
Notable Date(s)	

Name	
Address	
Phone	
Work Phone/Fax	
Email	
Notable Date(s)	

Name	
Address	
Phone	
Work Phone/Fax	
Email	
Notable Date(s)	

Name	
Address	
Phone	
Work Phone/Fax	
Email	
Notable Date(s)	

Name	
Address	
Phone	
Work Phone/Fax	
Email	
Notable Date(s)	

Name	
Address	
Phone	
Work Phone/Fax	
Email	
Notable Date(s)	

Name	
Address	
Phone	
Work Phone/Fax	
Email	
Notable Date(s)	

Name	
Address	
Phone	
Work Phone/Fax	
Email	
Notable Date(s)	

N

Name	
Address	
Phone	
Work Phone/Fax	
Email	
Notable Date(s)	

Name	
Address	
Phone	
Work Phone/Fax	
Email	
Notable Date(s)	

Name	
Address	
Phone	
Work Phone/Fax	
Email	
Notable Date(s)	

Name	
Address	
Phone	
Work Phone/Fax	
Email	
Notable Date(s)	

Name	
Address	
Phone	
Work Phone/Fax	
Email	
Notable Date(s)	

Name	
Address	
Phone	
Work Phone/Fax	
Email	
Notable Date(s)	

Name	
Address	
Phone	
Work Phone/Fax	
Email	
Notable Date(s)	

Name	
Address	
Phone	
Work Phone/Fax	
Email	
Notable Date(s)	

Name	
Address	
Phone	
Work Phone/Fax	
Email	
Notable Date(s)	

N

Name	
Address	
Phone	
Work Phone/Fax	
Email	
Notable Date(s)	

Name	
Address	
Phone	
Work Phone/Fax	
Email	
Notable Date(s)	

Name	
Address	
Phone	
Work Phone/Fax	
Email	
Notable Date(s)	

O

Name	
Address	
Phone	
Work Phone/Fax	
Email	
Notable Date(s)	

Name	
Address	
Phone	
Work Phone/Fax	
Email	
Notable Date(s)	

Name	
Address	
Phone	
Work Phone/Fax	
Email	
Notable Date(s)	

O

Name	
Address	
Phone	
Work Phone/Fax	
Email	
Notable Date(s)	

Name	
Address	
Phone	
Work Phone/Fax	
Email	
Notable Date(s)	

Name	
Address	
Phone	
Work Phone/Fax	
Email	
Notable Date(s)	

O

Name	
Address	
Phone	
Work Phone/Fax	
Email	
Notable Date(s)	

Name	
Address	
Phone	
Work Phone/Fax	
Email	
Notable Date(s)	

Name	
Address	
Phone	
Work Phone/Fax	
Email	
Notable Date(s)	

O

Name	
Address	
Phone	
Work Phone/Fax	
Email	
Notable Date(s)	

Name	
Address	
Phone	
Work Phone/Fax	
Email	
Notable Date(s)	

Name	
Address	
Phone	
Work Phone/Fax	
Email	
Notable Date(s)	

P

Name	
Address	
Phone	
Work Phone/Fax	
Email	
Notable Date(s)	

Name	
Address	
Phone	
Work Phone/Fax	
Email	
Notable Date(s)	

Name	
Address	
Phone	
Work Phone/Fax	
Email	
Notable Date(s)	

Name	
Address	
Phone	
Work Phone/Fax	
Email	
Notable Date(s)	

Name	
Address	
Phone	
Work Phone/Fax	
Email	
Notable Date(s)	

Name	
Address	
Phone	
Work Phone/Fax	
Email	
Notable Date(s)	

Name	
Address	
Phone	
Work Phone/Fax	
Email	
Notable Date(s)	

Name	
Address	
Phone	
Work Phone/Fax	
Email	
Notable Date(s)	

Name	
Address	
Phone	
Work Phone/Fax	
Email	
Notable Date(s)	

Name	
Address	
Phone	
Work Phone/Fax	
Email	
Notable Date(s)	

Name	
Address	
Phone	
Work Phone/Fax	
Email	
Notable Date(s)	

Name	
Address	
Phone	
Work Phone/Fax	
Email	
Notable Date(s)	

Q

Name	
Address	
Phone	
Work Phone/Fax	
Email	
Notable Date(s)	

Name	
Address	
Phone	
Work Phone/Fax	
Email	
Notable Date(s)	

Name	
Address	
Phone	
Work Phone/Fax	
Email	
Notable Date(s)	

Name	
Address	
Phone	
Work Phone/Fax	
Email	
Notable Date(s)	

Name	
Address	
Phone	
Work Phone/Fax	
Email	
Notable Date(s)	

Name	
Address	
Phone	
Work Phone/Fax	
Email	
Notable Date(s)	

Q

Name	
Address	
Phone	
Work Phone/Fax	
Email	
Notable Date(s)	

Name	
Address	
Phone	
Work Phone/Fax	
Email	
Notable Date(s)	

Name	
Address	
Phone	
Work Phone/Fax	
Email	
Notable Date(s)	

Name	
Address	
Phone	
Work Phone/Fax	
Email	
Notable Date(s)	

Name	
Address	
Phone	
Work Phone/Fax	
Email	
Notable Date(s)	

Name	
Address	
Phone	
Work Phone/Fax	
Email	
Notable Date(s)	

Name	
Address	
Phone	
Work Phone/Fax	
Email	
Notable Date(s)	

Name	
Address	
Phone	
Work Phone/Fax	
Email	
Notable Date(s)	

Name	
Address	
Phone	
Work Phone/Fax	
Email	
Notable Date(s)	

Name	
Address	
Phone	
Work Phone/Fax	
Email	
Notable Date(s)	

Name	
Address	
Phone	
Work Phone/Fax	
Email	
Notable Date(s)	

Name	
Address	
Phone	
Work Phone/Fax	
Email	
Notable Date(s)	

Name	
Address	
Phone	
Work Phone/Fax	
Email	
Notable Date(s)	

Name	
Address	
Phone	
Work Phone/Fax	
Email	
Notable Date(s)	

Name	
Address	
Phone	
Work Phone/Fax	
Email	
Notable Date(s)	

Name	
Address	
Phone	
Work Phone/Fax	
Email	
Notable Date(s)	

Name	
Address	
Phone	
Work Phone/Fax	
Email	
Notable Date(s)	

Name	
Address	
Phone	
Work Phone/Fax	
Email	
Notable Date(s)	

S

Name	
Address	
Phone	
Work Phone/Fax	
Email	
Notable Date(s)	

Name	
Address	
Phone	
Work Phone/Fax	
Email	
Notable Date(s)	

Name	
Address	
Phone	
Work Phone/Fax	
Email	
Notable Date(s)	

S

Name	
Address	
Phone	
Work Phone/Fax	
Email	
Notable Date(s)	

Name	
Address	
Phone	
Work Phone/Fax	
Email	
Notable Date(s)	

Name	
Address	
Phone	
Work Phone/Fax	
Email	
Notable Date(s)	

S

Name	
Address	
Phone	
Work Phone/Fax	
Email	
Notable Date(s)	

Name	
Address	
Phone	
Work Phone/Fax	
Email	
Notable Date(s)	

Name	
Address	
Phone	
Work Phone/Fax	
Email	
Notable Date(s)	

S

Name	
Address	
Phone	
Work Phone/Fax	
Email	
Notable Date(s)	

Name	
Address	
Phone	
Work Phone/Fax	
Email	
Notable Date(s)	

Name	
Address	
Phone	
Work Phone/Fax	
Email	
Notable Date(s)	

T

Name	
Address	
Phone	
Work Phone/Fax	
Email	
Notable Date(s)	

Name	
Address	
Phone	
Work Phone/Fax	
Email	
Notable Date(s)	

Name	
Address	
Phone	
Work Phone/Fax	
Email	
Notable Date(s)	

T

Name	
Address	
Phone	
Work Phone/Fax	
Email	
Notable Date(s)	

Name	
Address	
Phone	
Work Phone/Fax	
Email	
Notable Date(s)	

Name	
Address	
Phone	
Work Phone/Fax	
Email	
Notable Date(s)	

T

Name	
Address	
Phone	
Work Phone/Fax	
Email	
Notable Date(s)	

Name	
Address	
Phone	
Work Phone/Fax	
Email	
Notable Date(s)	

Name	
Address	
Phone	
Work Phone/Fax	
Email	
Notable Date(s)	

T

Name	
Address	
Phone	
Work Phone/Fax	
Email	
Notable Date(s)	

Name	
Address	
Phone	
Work Phone/Fax	
Email	
Notable Date(s)	

Name	
Address	
Phone	
Work Phone/Fax	
Email	
Notable Date(s)	

U

Name	
Address	
Phone	
Work Phone/Fax	
Email	
Notable Date(s)	

Name	
Address	
Phone	
Work Phone/Fax	
Email	
Notable Date(s)	

Name	
Address	
Phone	
Work Phone/Fax	
Email	
Notable Date(s)	

Name	
Address	
Phone	
Work Phone/Fax	
Email	
Notable Date(s)	

Name	
Address	
Phone	
Work Phone/Fax	
Email	
Notable Date(s)	

Name	
Address	
Phone	
Work Phone/Fax	
Email	
Notable Date(s)	

U

Name	
Address	
Phone	
Work Phone/Fax	
Email	
Notable Date(s)	

Name	
Address	
Phone	
Work Phone/Fax	
Email	
Notable Date(s)	

Name	
Address	
Phone	
Work Phone/Fax	
Email	
Notable Date(s)	

U

Name	
Address	
Phone	
Work Phone/Fax	
Email	
Notable Date(s)	

Name	
Address	
Phone	
Work Phone/Fax	
Email	
Notable Date(s)	

Name	
Address	
Phone	
Work Phone/Fax	
Email	
Notable Date(s)	

Name	
Address	
Phone	
Work Phone/Fax	
Email	
Notable Date(s)	

Name	
Address	
Phone	
Work Phone/Fax	
Email	
Notable Date(s)	

Name	
Address	
Phone	
Work Phone/Fax	
Email	
Notable Date(s)	

Name	
Address	
Phone	
Work Phone/Fax	
Email	
Notable Date(s)	

Name	
Address	
Phone	
Work Phone/Fax	
Email	
Notable Date(s)	

Name	
Address	
Phone	
Work Phone/Fax	
Email	
Notable Date(s)	

Name	
Address	
Phone	
Work Phone/Fax	
Email	
Notable Date(s)	

Name	
Address	
Phone	
Work Phone/Fax	
Email	
Notable Date(s)	

Name	
Address	
Phone	
Work Phone/Fax	
Email	
Notable Date(s)	

Name	
Address	
Phone	
Work Phone/Fax	
Email	
Notable Date(s)	

Name	
Address	
Phone	
Work Phone/Fax	
Email	
Notable Date(s)	

Name	
Address	
Phone	
Work Phone/Fax	
Email	
Notable Date(s)	

Name	
Address	
Phone	
Work Phone/Fax	
Email	
Notable Date(s)	

Name	
Address	
Phone	
Work Phone/Fax	
Email	
Notable Date(s)	

Name	
Address	
Phone	
Work Phone/Fax	
Email	
Notable Date(s)	

Name	
Address	
Phone	
Work Phone/Fax	
Email	
Notable Date(s)	
Name	
Address	
Phone	
Work Phone/Fax	
Email	
Notable Date(s)	
Name	
Address	
Phone	
Work Phone/Fax	
Email	
Notable Date(s)	

Name	
Address	
Phone	
Work Phone/Fax	
Email	
Notable Date(s)	

Name	
Address	
Phone	
Work Phone/Fax	
Email	
Notable Date(s)	

Name	
Address	
Phone	
Work Phone/Fax	
Email	
Notable Date(s)	

Name	
Address	
Phone	
Work Phone/Fax	
Email	
Notable Date(s)	

Name	
Address	
Phone	
Work Phone/Fax	
Email	
Notable Date(s)	

Name	
Address	
Phone	
Work Phone/Fax	
Email	
Notable Date(s)	

Name	
Address	
Phone	
Work Phone/Fax	
Email	
Notable Date(s)	

Name	
Address	
Phone	
Work Phone/Fax	
Email	
Notable Date(s)	

Name	
Address	
Phone	
Work Phone/Fax	
Email	
Notable Date(s)	

Name	
Address	
Phone	
Work Phone/Fax	
Email	
Notable Date(s)	

Name	
Address	
Phone	
Work Phone/Fax	
Email	
Notable Date(s)	

Name	
Address	
Phone	
Work Phone/Fax	
Email	
Notable Date(s)	

Name	
Address	
Phone	
Work Phone/Fax	
Email	
Notable Date(s)	

Name	
Address	
Phone	
Work Phone/Fax	
Email	
Notable Date(s)	

Name	
Address	
Phone	
Work Phone/Fax	
Email	
Notable Date(s)	

Name	
Address	
Phone	
Work Phone/Fax	
Email	
Notable Date(s)	

Name	
Address	
Phone	
Work Phone/Fax	
Email	
Notable Date(s)	

Name	
Address	
Phone	
Work Phone/Fax	
Email	
Notable Date(s)	

Y

Name	
Address	
Phone	
Work Phone/Fax	
Email	
Notable Date(s)	

Name	
Address	
Phone	
Work Phone/Fax	
Email	
Notable Date(s)	

Name	
Address	
Phone	
Work Phone/Fax	
Email	
Notable Date(s)	

Name	
Address	
Phone	
Work Phone/Fax	
Email	
Notable Date(s)	

Name	
Address	
Phone	
Work Phone/Fax	
Email	
Notable Date(s)	

Name	
Address	
Phone	
Work Phone/Fax	
Email	
Notable Date(s)	

Y

Name	
Address	
Phone	
Work Phone/Fax	
Email	
Notable Date(s)	

Name	
Address	
Phone	
Work Phone/Fax	
Email	
Notable Date(s)	

Name	
Address	
Phone	
Work Phone/Fax	
Email	
Notable Date(s)	

Name	
Address	
Phone	
Work Phone/Fax	
Email	
Notable Date(s)	

Name	
Address	
Phone	
Work Phone/Fax	
Email	
Notable Date(s)	

Name	
Address	
Phone	
Work Phone/Fax	
Email	
Notable Date(s)	

Z

Name	
Address	
Phone	
Work Phone/Fax	
Email	
Notable Date(s)	

Name	
Address	
Phone	
Work Phone/Fax	
Email	
Notable Date(s)	

Name	
Address	
Phone	
Work Phone/Fax	
Email	
Notable Date(s)	

Name	
Address	
Phone	
Work Phone/Fax	
Email	
Notable Date(s)	

Name	
Address	
Phone	
Work Phone/Fax	
Email	
Notable Date(s)	

Name	
Address	
Phone	
Work Phone/Fax	
Email	
Notable Date(s)	

Z

Name	
Address	
Phone	
Work Phone/Fax	
Email	
Notable Date(s)	

Name	
Address	
Phone	
Work Phone/Fax	
Email	
Notable Date(s)	

Name	
Address	
Phone	
Work Phone/Fax	
Email	
Notable Date(s)	

Name	
Address	
Phone	
Work Phone/Fax	
Email	
Notable Date(s)	

Name	
Address	
Phone	
Work Phone/Fax	
Email	
Notable Date(s)	

Name	
Address	
Phone	
Work Phone/Fax	
Email	
Notable Date(s)	

Made in the USA
Monee, IL
14 December 2021